PASTELS

by Mari Bolte   illustrated by Pamela Becker

Content Consultant:
Robert A. Williams
Artist and Teacher
Instructor of Commercial and Technical Art
South Central College, North Mankato, Minnesota

CAPSTONE PRESS
a capstone imprint

Snap Books are published by Capstone Press,
1710 Roe Crest Drive, North Mankato, Minnesota 56003.
www.capstonepub.com

Library of Congress Cataloging-in-Publication Data
Bolte, Mari.
  Pastels / By Mari Bolte ; illustrated by Pamela Becker.
     pages cm. — (Snap books. Paint it)
  Summary: "Step-by-step guides show how to create a variety of projects using
pastels"—Provided by publisher.
  ISBN 978-1-4765-3111-3 (library binding)
  ISBN 978-1-4765-3569-2 (ebook PDF)
1. Pastel drawing—Technique—Juvenile literature. I. Becker, Pamela. II. Title.
  NC880.B65 2014
  741.2'35—dc23   2013005396

Designer: Bobbie Nuytten
Production Specialist: Laura Manthe

Photo Credits:
Illustrations by Pamela Becker; All photos by Capstone Studio and
Pamela Becker except the following: Getty Images: Gareth Cattermole,
31 (bottom right); Newscom: prn, 26 (bottom right); Shutterstock:
CGissemann, 24 (left), Christopher Hall, 7 (bottom), Nino Cavalier, 1,
2 (bottom), 31 (top)

Printed in the United States of America in
Stevens Point, Wisconsin
032013   007227WZF13

Table of Contents

IN YOUR ART BOX

Pastels don't come in a tube and aren't applied with a brush. But these smudgeable, smearable, grown-up crayons are the perfect painting medium. Because they use pigment, pastels are considered paints. In fact, these were the very first paints used by people. Give these sticks of pigment a try and make them first in your art book.

PASTELS

Many people find pastels to be the easiest paint medium to work with. Pastels don't need time to dry, and no special tools are required. They don't crack, darken, or change color over time. They can be applied in any order, so there's no need to paint light to dark. And they can be used on almost any kind of paper.

Although pastels are the most basic paint medium, they come in many varieties. The color wheel above shows soft pastels (outer circle), oil pastels (middle circle), and pastel pencils (inner circle).

Soft Pastels: Soft pastels are sold as thick sticks. They are made of pigment mixed with binder and white coloring. Soft pastels have the smallest amount of binder. They draw soft, easy-to-smudge lines.

Hard Pastels: Hard pastels are sold as thin sticks. They are made with more binder. This means that colors may fade. They can be sharpened and draw thin, even lines.

Pastel Pencils: Pastel pencils are like regular pencils, but with cores of pastel instead of lead. They can be sharpened. Pastel pencils are good for narrow lines and detail work. Like hard pastels, they can fade over time.

Oil Pastels: Oil pastels are sold as thick sticks wrapped in paper. They are sometimes called wax crayons. Oil pastels are made of pigment mixed with an oil or wax binder. They make a thick, greasy line that can be smudged with turpentine or mineral spirits.

Chalk: Chalk is made by mixing natural minerals with an oil binder. Artist's chalk is different from the chalk used on chalkboard, which contains no binder.

Paints and Pigments

All paints are made up of a pigment and a binder. Pigments are dry, colored powders. They can be natural or artificial. They can come from plants, animals, the earth, or a lab. Pigment is what colors all painting mediums. The only difference between paint mediums is the binder that is used.

Binders are adhesive liquids that hold pigment. Pigment reacts differently depending on the binder that is used. This is why one color of oil paint looks different than the same color of watercolor paint.

Pastels are made with pure pigment and just a little a binding agent. This is why they are said to be the purest paints.

TIPS AND TECHNIQUES

Pastels are easy to use and easy to experiment with. Grab a few sticks, start sketching, and get creative!

~Draw with the tip of the pastel stick. Use the side of the stick to paint.

~Use a sharp knife to sharpen pastels. Sandpaper is a good tool to shape the pastels into points.

~Tap loose powder off your paper as you work. This will help keep your workspace clean. It will also help additional layers of color cling to the paper.

~Limit direct skin contact with hazardous pigments, especially if you use professional grade pastels. Try to use paper, blending sticks, or cloth to blend instead of your finger whenever possible. This prevents toxic materials from entering through your skin.

Thumbnails are a great way to experiment with pastels. Miniatures that you really like can be blown up to full-sized projects later.

~To clean pastels, wipe each stick with a paper towel. To give a thorough cleaning, place a handful of cornmeal in a container with a lid. Add a few pastels at a time. Shake gently for a minute or two or until pastels are completely clean.

~Pastels can smear easily. Spray finished pieces with fixative or frame them under glass. Follow all safety instructions while using fixative.

~When using pastels, work in a well-ventilated area. Gloves and a mask give extra protection from pastel dust. Be sure to wash up well afterward!

Many simple techniques can be used with pastels. Practice blending and layering until you feel comfortable working with each kind of pastel.

COLOR PALETTE

Pastels can be purchased in individual sticks or in sets of six, 12, 24, or more. Before buying the biggest set, think about how much you plan on using them. Think about storage too. Pastels must be kept clean and organized. If you plan on traveling with your pastels, consider weight. Pastels are heavy. The more you buy, the more you'll have to carry with you.

Try to buy pastels with natural pigments, such as ochres, umbers, and oxides. They are less likely to fade over time.

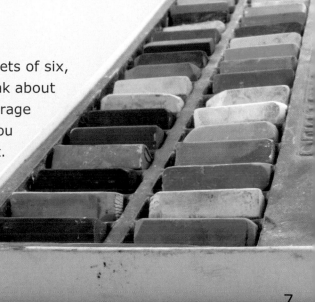

Rub It In

Get started with simple experimenting. Grab some everyday blending tools and a cup of water. Then find out what you can do with a simple box of pastels.

Wet and Dry

Your first rainbow will explore how soft pastels blend using brushes. How do they behave when dry? How do they behave when wet?

1 Draw a rainbow across your paper. Blend half the rainbow with a wet paintbrush.

2 Blend the other half of the rainbow with a dry paintbrush.

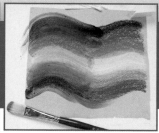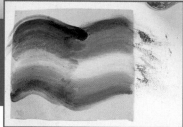

Soft Swabs

The object you use for blending can change the way your pastels look.

1 Blend the rainbow lines with a dry cotton swab.

2 Reblend the rainbow lines with a wet cotton swab. The wet lines will dry lighter than the others.

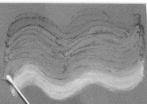

Blended 'bow

A makeup sponge can soften pastels. The colors flow together and become light and airy. Compare this rainbow to the one blended with the cotton swab.

1 Draw dark, rich lines onto your pastel paper.

2 Blend the colors with a makeup sponge. Notice how the sponge softens the lines.

 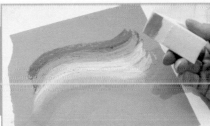 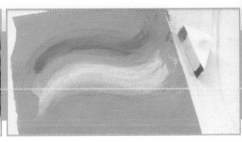

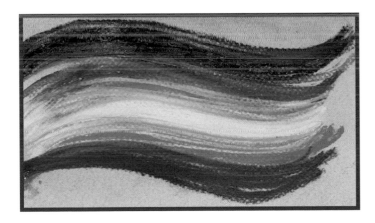

Painted Pastels

This rainbow shows another way water affects pastels.

1 Wet your pastel paper. For an even coat of water, use a thick, soft paintbrush.

2 Draw over the wet paper with pastels. Notice how the lines hold their shape.

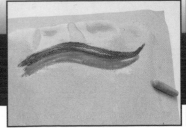  

In The Lines

Play with pastels to paint this colorful prism. Each color stripe shows a different technique to use with oil pastels.

1 Mask the edges of the paper and tape to your work station.

2 Lightly sketch the prism onto the paper.

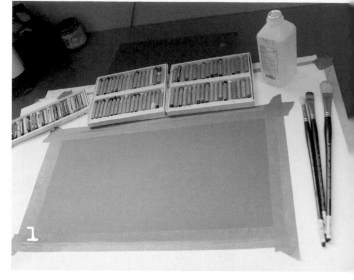

The kind of paper used can change how the final painting looks. Colored paper may show through the pigment. It can also help the pastel colors pop. Textured paper gives the pastels something to grab onto. The more textured the paper, the deeper the pigments appear.

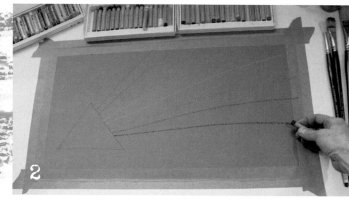

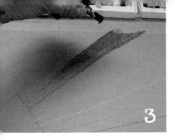

3 Begin with the purple stripe. Color the stripe using fine parallel lines. Then add a second layer of lines going a slightly different direction to create cross-hatching.

4 Color the next line blue. Use a paintbrush to smear the line with rubbing alcohol.

5 Color the next stripe light green. Then set a cold cookie sheet over the paper (or put the paper in the freezer.)

While the paper is chilling, warm the end of a dark green pastel by holding it against a heating pad or coffee cup warmer. Use the hot pastel stick to color over the light green stripe on the cold paper. The pastel should create a thick, saturated dark green stripe over the light green.

6 Color the next stripe light yellow. Blend part of a dark yellow pastel stick with linseed oil. Paint over the light yellow with the thinned dark yellow.

7 Brush the next stripe with linseed oil. Then color directly over the oil with an orange pastel stick.

8 Use glue to design a pattern over the next stripe. Let dry completely. Color over the dried glue with a red-orange pastel stick.

9 Color the red stripe by moving your pastel stick in tight circles.

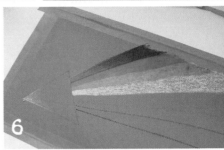

Sharp Points

Give your art a fine point with pastel pencils. Most artists find pastel pencils easy to hold and less messy than regular pastels. Compare the many ways pastel pencils can be used by lining them up as a crafty chevron.

1 Use a ruler, pencil, and scissors to measure and cut out rectangles from white and colored paper.

2 Decorate each rectangle using a different color or technique.

3 Once you're done experimenting, arrange the strips into a rainbow chevron pattern. Glue the pieces together onto a piece of paper.

Glazes and Scumbles

A **glaze** is a transparent layer of dark paint over light opaque paint. Glazes give paintings the appearance of depth.

A **scumble** is a layer of light paint applied over darker paint. Scumbling is one way to add light to paintings.

Try some of these techniques to get familiar with pastel pencils!

~ Blend with water, rubbing alcohol, or linseed oil

~ Blend with cotton swabs, paintbrushes, or blending sticks

~ Use white, colored, or textured paper

~ Layer different shades of the same colors together

~ Layer different colors

~ Gently rub the side of the pastel over a colored base. This will blend and soften the layers, creating a glaze or scumble.

~ Paint using cross-hatching. Have the first layer of lines be one color. Paint the top layer another color.

~ Paint thin lines of one color. Then paint thin lines of another color going the same way on top of the first lines. This will create a feathering effect.

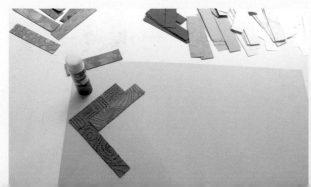

Triple Rainbows

Black paper is the perfect tool to let pastels shine. Use what you learned about the different pastel types to create a larger-than-life masterpiece.

Sanded black pastel paper will hold the most pigment. The textured surface gives pigment something to grab onto.

2

1 Begin by drawing some large, flowing lines across the paper. Try to use the entire paper.

2 Continue adding to the flowing lines. Use a variety of pastel types. (The blue dots are oils, the orange and green lines are medium, and the red lines are pencil.)

3 Create layers with oil pastels.

4 Build color by creating soft pastel rainbows. Then blend them together.

5 Blend regular pastels around and into the oil circles.

6 Use pastel pencils to create sharp lines between contrasting colors.

7 Don't be afraid to change the direction and flow of the lines. Let the lines come naturally.

Make a mistake? Grab an old toothbrush. Lightly brush over whatever you want to erase.

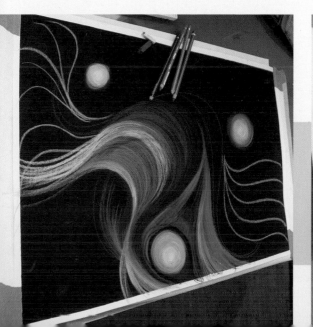

Let some of the black paper show through. This will create natural shading and dimension.

15

Perspectives

Create interest in your art by drawing a bright focal point. A painting's focal point pulls the viewer's eye right to it. Take a lesson in perspective. Soon you'll have a piece of art that people can't stop staring at.

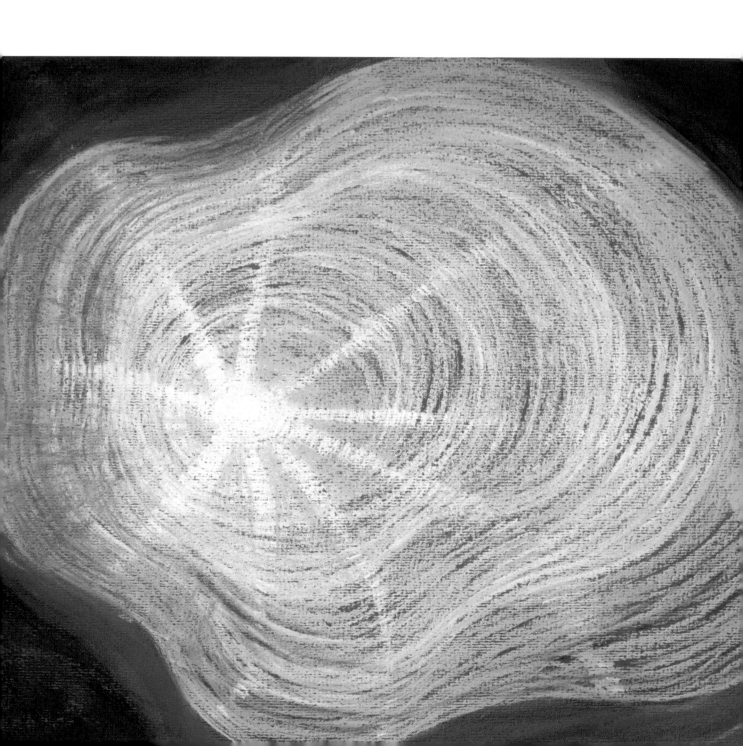

1 Use tape to mask off a square on your paper.

2 Choose the focal point for your masterpiece. Mark it with a light dot.

3 Begin sketching circles around your focal point to create a tunnel.

4 Give the tunnel outer edges. The edges should be a different color.

5 Draw perspective lines coming from the center of the tunnel. The lines will give your tunnel a more 3D feel.

6 Continue adding "walls" to your tunnel.

7 Add highlights to the light at the end of the tunnel.

8 Add highlights and shadows to the tunnel walls.

9 As a final step, darken the outside edges of the tunnel. Remove tape when completely finished.

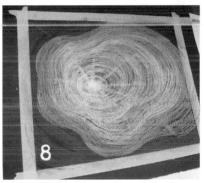

Make sure your colored paper was dyed with permanent pigments. This ensures that the colors won't fade.

Scratch-Off

Scratch art, or sgraffito, can create bold decoration or subtle accent. Create a hidden rainbow. Then reveal your design one scratch at a time. Scratching off that last layer can be fun and rewarding!

1 Create an abstract pattern using oil pastels. Use a heavyweight paper and press hard.

2 For the best effect, continue layering until you have a thick base of oil pastel.

3 Cover your drawing with a thick layer of black oil pastel. The black layer should almost cover the base layer completely.

4 Choose a tool for scratching. Some good scratching tools include:
- teeth from a comb
- clay loops
- toothpicks
- pens with the ink removed
- steel wool
- paintbrush handle

5 Scratch your design into the black oil pastel.

Scratchboard, gessoed board, or heavyweight pastel paper are best for this project.

For greatest effect, let your colored layer set overnight before adding the black layer.

Use a vacuum to pick up the bits of scratched-off pastel as you go.

Batik Heat

Get inspired by batik! Batik is a fabric dying technique from Indonesia. Hot wax is applied to cloth. Then the fabric is dyed. The wax is removed, leaving behind a pattern or design. White glue and soft pastels are safer and easier than wax and dye. Shine some light on this sensational style with a soft sun.

Resist Painting

Batik is a form of resist painting. The glue resists paint and pigment, allowing the plain paper to show through. Tape, crayons and wax, masking fluid, and glue all work well for resist painting.

1 Lightly sketch your design onto your paper. Use a pastel or colored pencil in a similar color to your paper so the lines won't show later.

2 Trace your design with white glue. Start from the inside and work your way toward the paper's edges.

3 When you are happy with your glue design, let it dry overnight.

4 Add color using soft pastels. Start coloring the center and work your way out. This will prevent smearing.

5 Paint the corners. Use a makeup sponge to blend inward. Paint inside swirls, but let the blending color the outside.

Soft Edges

Take advantage of the butcher paper's natural colors tone and test out bold, fantastic colors. A sweeping piece of art with no hard lines or edges will let this fantasy horse gallop across the page.

1 Tape the edges of your paper to keep it flat.

2 Loosely sketch the form of the horse. Try to feel the horse's breath, movement, and life in your sketch.

3 Begin adding highlights and reflections on the horse's body. Soft pastels work well for this.

4 Draw the horse's features in more detail. Use pastel pencils to add more definition. Follow and build on the highlights you drew in the previous step.

5 Add more color to the horse, giving it more dimension and shape.

6 Add the horse's mane and muscles.

7 Finish with white highlights to give your horse a sunkissed look.

8 Drag pastels flat across the paper for a scumbling effect.

Butcher paper is good for more than sketching. It can also be used to protect your work surface. Tape a piece of butcher paper down to keep your table paint and pigment free.

Displaying Your Art

Although time does not cause pastels to fade, light will. Protect your finished pastel art by matting and framing it. Both matting and glass protect your art from dust and dirt, and prevent smudging.

Fixatives help "set" the pastels. They ensure the pastels cannot be brushed off. Fixatives can be hazardous, however. Wear a mask while spraying, and use only in a well-ventilated area. Be careful not to overuse fixative. Too much can dissolve pigment and change your painting's colors.

Butcher paper can be found at restaurant, teaching, and art supply stores.

Color Matching

Challenge yourself and take cookies and milk to the next level of sweetness. Use your artistic eye to pick out the base colors in a photograph. Then stick to them! Using only a few hues can be more freeing than having to choose from an entire rainbow. If sweets aren't your thing, don't get discouraged—any photo will do.

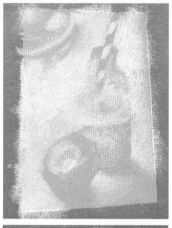

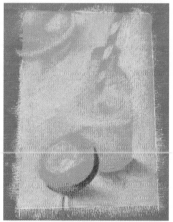

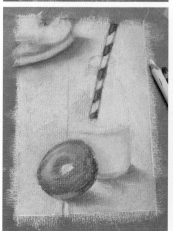

If you have a hard time matching colors, look online. There are many free tools that will help you pull colors directly from your photo. A visit to a paint store might help too. Check out the wall of paint swatches to find the right shades of color.

1 Select a photograph. Try to find a photo that has only four or five colors throughout.

2 Tape your paper down. Mask off an area of a similar shape and size to your photograph.

3 Use a gray pastel to start your sketch. Look carefully at shape and scale. Try to keep your sketch as close to the photograph as possible.

4 Begin filling in the basic shapes of the donut and straw, working toward matching the original photograph's color.

5 Blend the tan and brown pastels to give the milk a rich, creamy appearance.

6 Continue adding layers of color and shading. Give the donut more details, including a shiny glaze and scattering of sprinkles.

The gray underlayer is called grisaille. This layer establishes the painting's light and dark tones. It also gives the finished painting depth and dimension.

Pop Warhol

Celebrate pop culture with Pop Art. Color familiar objects with bright hues. Get inspired by movie stars, comic book characters, logos, and magazine ads.

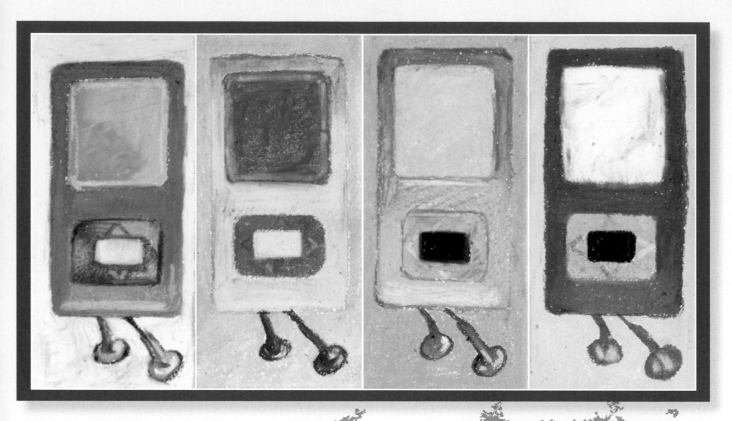

Andy Warhol

Andy Warhol (1928–1987) was an American artist active during the Pop Art movement (1950s–1960s.) He is probably most famous for his silkscreen printing technique. This technique made it easy to mass produce art. His screenprints of Marilyn Monroe, Elvis Presley, Jackie Onassis, and soup cans are now famous icons.

1 Divide a piece of pastel paper into four sections.

2 Print out a picture of your MP3 player, or sketch it onto a piece of paper.

3 Place your MP3 player on top of a piece of transfer paper. Place both papers onto a section of your pastel paper. Use a pen or mechanical pencil to trace the MP3 player onto your pastel paper.

4 Repeat step 3 until each section of your paper has an MP3 player in it.

Transfer paper is a special kind of paper coated with a layer of graphite. Tracing over the graphite transfers the image to the pastel paper.

5 Color each section with oil pastels. Try different color combinations for each section. Use bright colors with high contrasts.

For help choosing colors, do an Internet search for "pop art color palettes." Many Warhol-inspired palettes are available for comparison.

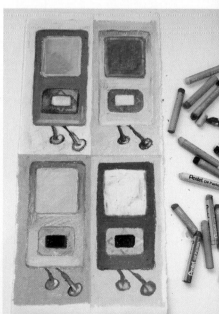

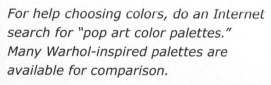

Street Sense

Never feel limited to flat pages in a studio! Get outside and explore the world of 3D chalk art. Artists around the world are taking to the street and bringing realistic drawings to life.

Get the OK before you start! Check with business owners, parks and recreation departments, or homeowners before sketching on the sidewalk.

Full-time chalk artists use professional-quality soft pastels. You will go through a lot of pastels this way. Chalk pastels are a cheaper choice for the beginner. Start there, and work your way up as your art improves.

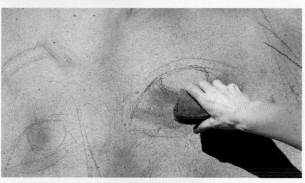

Use a grid to keep your layout to scale. Remember that your drawing will be longer than normal. The farthest-away points will be wider too.

1 Choose a location where you can play with perspective. Try to pick a place that's out of the way and has little traffic.

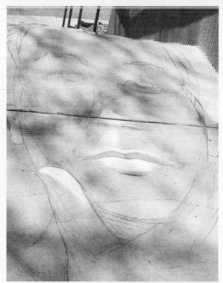

2 Take a photo of the location from where your viewer will stand.

3 Sketch your photograph onto a piece of paper. Use this as your layout as you decide what to draw.

4 Use charcoal to sketch your layout onto the sidewalk. Keep a bucket of water and a sponge nearby to fix any mistakes.

5 Choose cool colors to fill in shadows and warm colors as highlights. Try to use contrasting colors. Make sure you have enough of every color to fill in the entire area.

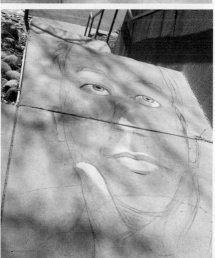

Image editing software can be a great tool. Some can show you how to draw your image to add perspective and dimension. There are also special grids online. Search for "3D anamorphic image grid."

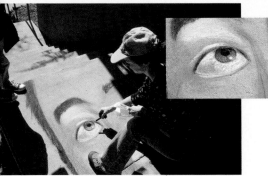

6 Add shadows with blue pastels. Work light to dark, blending colors together. Try to start in the center and work your way toward the edges.

7 Continue building color and shading with yellows, oranges, and greens.

8 Color the area around the face and add final highlights. Then photograph your finished work!

Step away from your drawing often. This will ensure that the drawing stays balanced and to scale.

Tips For Success

- Use an old pillow or knee pads. These will save wear and tear on your knees and clothes.

- Wear old clothes! You'll be covered in pastel dust.

- Rags, plastic foam, and bits of carpet are great blending tools.

- Plan to paint all day. This is a big piece of artwork and will take a while to finish.

- Take photographs of your finished work! It might not be there tomorrow.

- Some chalk artists "prime" the sidewalk with a thin layer of tempera paint. The paint helps the chalk stick, and washes away with rain.

- If the weather turns against you, try covering your art with plastic sheeting and duct tape. It may help save your masterpiece.

Kurt Wenner

American Kurt Wenner (1971–) invented 3D pavement art in 1984. In 1982 he quit his job as a NASA illustrator to study Renaissance art. He saw that Renaissance painters used perspective to create optical illusions. Wenner borrowed that idea. When viewed from the wrong angle, Wenner's paintings look strange. But when seen from the right spot, they pop or sink from the ground.

Read More

Anholt, Laurence. *Anholt's Artists Activity Book*.
Hauppauge, N.Y.: Barrons Educational Series,
Inc., 2012.

Frisch-Schmoll, Joy. *Still Lifes*. Brushes with Greatness.
Mankato, Minn.: Creative Paperbacks, 2013.

Finger, Brad. *13 American Artists Children Should Know*.
New York: Prestel Pub., 2010.

Internet Sites

FactHound offers a safe, fun way to find Internet sites
related to this book. All of the sites on FactHound have
been researched by our staff.

Here's all you do:

Visit *www.facthound.com*

Type in this code: 9781476531113

 Check out projects, games and lots more at
www.capstonekids.com

Author Bio

Mari Bolte is an author of children's books and
a lover of art. She lives in southern Minnesota
with her husband, daughter, and two wiener
dogs. A degree in creative writing has taught her
the value of fine writing. Parenthood has made
her a purveyor of fine art, with specializations in
sidewalk chalk, washable markers, and glitter glue.

Illustrator Bio

Pamela Becker, a Rhode Island School of Design alumni,
enjoys the challenge of taking on projects that expand her
knowledge of the world and of herself. She has traveled
extensively studying mask making, mythology and dance,
which infuses her art with the patina of diversity.